Property Management
Maximizing Wealth in Real Estate Rentals

Table of Contents

1. Introduction 1
2. Understanding Real Estate as an Investment 2
    2.1. The Mechanism behind Real Estate Investing 2
    2.2. Choosing the Right Property for Investment 3
    2.3. Financing your Real Estate Investment 3
    2.4. Understanding Rent Calculation and Yield Analysis 4
    2.5. Appreciating the Tax Implications 4
    2.6. Managing the Risks 5
    2.7. Nurturing your Real Estate Portfolio 5
3. Essential Principles of Property Management 7
    3.1. Understand the Real Estate Market 7
    3.2. Financial Management 7
    3.3. Legal Compliance 8
    3.4. Tenant Management 8
    3.5. Property Maintenance 8
    3.6. Strategic Marketing 8
    3.7. Streamlining Operations 9
4. Building a Fiscally Balanced Portfolio 10
    4.1. How to Grow Your Portfolio 10
    4.2. Building a Diverse Portfolio 11
    4.3. The Financial Side of Things 11
    4.4. Future-Proofing Your Portfolio 12
5. The Art of Attracting and Retaining Tenants 13
    5.1. Knowing the Local Rental Market 13
    5.2. Marketing Your Property 13
    5.3. Making Impressions Count 14
    5.4. Screening Your Tenants 14
    5.5. Cultivating Strong Landlord-Tenant Relationships 14

5.6. Regular Maintenance and Improvements 15

5.7. Renewing Lease Agreements 15

6. Demystifying Property Maintenance and Renovation 17

6.1. The Basics of Property Maintenance 17

7. Reactive maintenance 18

8. Preventive maintenance 19

8.1. Hiring Property Maintenance Services 19

8.2. Tenant's Role in Property Maintenance 19

8.3. Leveraging Technology for Property Maintenance 20

8.4. When Renovations are Necessary 20

8.5. The Renovation Process 21

8.6. Renovation Payoffs 21

9. Effective Legal Practices and Rental Laws 23

9.1. Landlord-Tenant Laws 23

9.2. Eviction Laws 24

9.3. Fair Housing Act 24

9.4. Americans with Disabilities Act 25

9.5. Property Maintenance Laws 25

9.6. The Importance of Legal Assistance 25

10. The Role of Technology in Property Management 27

10.1. Digital Marketing and Property Advertising 27

10.2. Online Tenant Applications and Screening 28

10.3. Property Management Software 28

10.4. Use of AI and Chatbots 29

10.5. IoT and Smart Home Technology 29

11. Risk Management and Insurance Essentials 31

11.1. Risk Management Essentials 31

11.2. Insurance Essentials 32

12. Exploring the Power of Real Estate Tax Benefits 34

12.1. Understanding the Basics 34

12.2. Navigating Capital Gains Tax 34

12.3. Unpacking Depreciation 35

12.4. Mortgage Interest and Other Expense Deductions 35

12.5. Real Estate Professional Status (REPS) 36

12.6. Utilizing the Passive Activity Loss Rule 36

12.7. Utilizing a Self-Directed IRA 36

12.8. Opportunity Zones 36

13. Strategies for Portfolio Expansion and Profit Maximization 38

13.1. Market Research 38

13.2. Property-Type Consideration 38

13.3. Financial Management 39

13.4. Long-Term Planning 39

13.5. Profit Maximization Strategies 40

13.6. Conclusion 40

Chapter 1. Introduction

Welcome to the "Property Management: Maximizing Wealth in Real Estate Rentals" special report where we make owning rental properties not only accessible but also vivaciously rewarding. Open the door to an industry buzzing with opportunity, even for those who aren't real estate gurus. This report is designed to energize your financial dreams, offering tangible insights into successfully managing your property, attracting tenants, and boosting profits from your real estate investments. Whether you're new to the rental market or a seasoned landlord looking to expand your portfolio, you don't want to miss out on this special report. It's your key to turning bricks and mortar into a goldmine! So, rev up those profit engines and prepare to sky-rocket your wealth through rental real estate in ways you never imagined possible. Ready to leap into your lucrative future? Let's get started!

Chapter 2. Understanding Real Estate as an Investment

The fundamental principle behind real estate as an investment is rather straightforward: acquire a property, perhaps spruce it up with a few renovations, find a suitable tenant who will pay rent over an agreed period, and - voila! - You have a cash-generating asset. But, of course, like any worthwhile endeavor, the devil is in the details. It is those details we'll meticulously delve into, demystifying the inner workings of this lucrative segment of the investment world, and positioning you for maximum returns.

2.1. The Mechanism behind Real Estate Investing

Real estate generates income in two primary ways. The first is through rental yield – the monthly rent you receive from tenants – and the second is capital appreciation, the increase in the property's value over time. While rental yields provide steady monthly returns and help cover operational costs, capital appreciation offers significant returns when the property is sold.

Property prices increase due to a combination of factors including economic growth, infrastructure development, and urbanization. For example, the construction of a new highway, shopping complex, or school in the vicinity of your rental property can dramatically increase its value. But remember, property values can also fall due to various factors such as recessions, high-interest rates, or unfavorable changes in the neighborhood.

2.2. Choosing the Right Property for Investment

Before investing in any property, it's crucial to evaluate potential returns. Consider the location, demand for rentals, the condition of the property, and the cost of any required renovations. Furthermore, investigate the history of property values in that area and future development plans. It's equally important to consider the type of property, whether residential, commercial, or industrial, as they each have different risks and returns.

Residential rental properties are often the easiest entry point for new investors. They require less capital up-front, and the rental market is typically more stable. Commercial properties can generate higher yields but also come with added complexities and risks, such as longer vacant periods between tenants.

2.3. Financing your Real Estate Investment

Funding is a significant consideration in real estate investing. While cash purchases eliminate the cost of interest, they also tie up a substantial amount of capital in one asset. On the other hand, leveraging – borrowing to invest – allows you to acquire more properties and maximize your potential returns.

However, keep in mind that debt increases risk. In the event of a market downturn or prolonged vacancy periods, you'll need to ensure you can cover your loan repayments. Proper financial planning is essential to sustain and grow your real estate portfolio over the long term.

2.4. Understanding Rent Calculation and Yield Analysis

Calculating rental yield is a crucial step in assessing the profitability of a property. To do so, you need to divide the gross annual rent by the property's total cost and multiply by 100.

[formula] Gross yield = annual rental income / total investment * 100 **[end formula]**

An even more useful measure is net yield, which accounts for operational expenses such as maintenance, property management fees, insurance, and taxes.

[formula] Net yield = (annual rental income - annual expenses) / total investment * 100 **[end formula]**

Both these measures can be used to compare different properties and markets to make informed investment decisions.

2.5. Appreciating the Tax Implications

Owning rental property comes with both tax benefits and obligations. The rent you receive is taxable income, but you can also deduct a number of expenses to reduce your tax liability. These deductions typically include property tax, mortgage interest, insurance, maintenance costs, and depreciation. Professional tax advice is highly recommended to maximize your benefits and avoid potential pitfalls.

One potential challenge is capital gains tax, which applies when you sell a property for more than you paid for it. This tax rate often depends on how long you owned the property and your overall income.

2.6. Managing the Risks

While real estate can provide compelling returns, it is not without risk. Market fluctuations, property damage, problematic tenants, unexpected maintenance expenses, and changes to tax laws can all impact your profitability. It's essential to understand, anticipate, and prepare for these risks.

Having a strong lease agreement, obtaining appropriate insurance, maintaining a cash reserve for emergencies, conducting regular property inspections, and staying updated with market trends and tax laws can significantly mitigate these risks.

2.7. Nurturing your Real Estate Portfolio

Successful property investment is about more than just buying a property and collecting rent; it's about nurturing your investment over time. Regular maintenance and improvements can increase your rental income and property value. Staying responsive to tenant needs can foster long-term, trouble-free tenancies. Regular market analysis can provide insights into when to buy more properties or dispose of underperforming assets.

Remember, real estate investing is a long-term commitment. It requires patience, diligence, and continuous learning. But with the right approach, it can be one of the most rewarding paths to wealth creation, leading you up the stairs to your very own financial heaven.

Ultimately, understanding real estate as an investment is about understanding the opportunities and appropriately navigating the complexities. Challenges are inherent, but armed with this knowledge and commitment, you're now better positioned to turn your property investment dreams into reality, one brick at a time.

Chapter 3. Essential Principles of Property Management

Before delving into the intricacies of property management, it is important to understand that successful property management stems from the adept application of a set of universal principles. These principles serve as the guiding light that shapes the actions and decisions made in the realm of rental real estate. Let's explore these principles in detail.

3.1. Understand the Real Estate Market

Gaining a deep understanding of the real estate market is pivotal. It is the bedrock upon which all investment decisions should be based. Understand market dynamics, local laws and regulations, demand and supply ratios, and how they impact property values and rental rates. Keep an eye on market trends, and harness the power of research to stay informed about the current market conditions and future growth prospects.

3.2. Financial Management

Financial management includes but is not limited to rent collection, budgeting, record keeping, taxation, and profit calculation. In essence, it's about the timely collection of rents, prudent spending, and strategic investment to improve the property's value. Effectively managing your finances will result in a healthy cash flow, which is a primary aim of investing in rental real estate.

3.3. Legal Compliance

You must ensure compliance with local and federal housing laws and regulations. Clear understanding of landlord-tenant laws, zoning laws, fair housing laws, and other relevant legislation is paramount, and it ensures that you protect your investment while respecting tenants' rights. Besides, the punitive nature of such laws means non-compliance can lead to hefty fines, lawsuits or, worse, loss of your property.

3.4. Tenant Management

Tenants are the lifeblood of your rental property investment. Successful tenant management entails a range of activities from the selection of suitable tenants, ensuring tenant retention, timely conflict resolution, to setting and regulating reasonable rent rates and lease terms. Cultivating good relations with your tenant can result in reliable revenue streams and improve the overall value of your property.

3.5. Property Maintenance

Preservation of the physical condition of the rental property is crucial. Systematic property maintenance, including regular inspections and timely repairs, safeguards the property's value, keeps tenants satisfied and can even justify rent increases.

3.6. Strategic Marketing

Investing in systematic and targeted marketing efforts could attract quality tenants. Strategic marketing includes advertising the property, using digital marketing techniques like SEO and social media, and staging the property to attract potential tenants. Remember, a vacant property is a financial liability, and effective marketing strategies can help you avoid prolonged vacancies.

3.7. Streamlining Operations

Optimization and streamlining of your property management processes is key. Leverage technology to automate tasks such as rent collection, contract management, workload management, and property inspection. This will help you save on costs, time, and effort, allowing you to focus more on strategic planning and decision-making.

Each of these principles is integral to robust property management and ought to be a crucial part of your property management strategy. Remember, effective property management is not just adhering to these principles in isolation but their adept application in unison. They are interlinked, and success in one aspect can set you up for overall success.

Now, armed with a solid understanding of these principles, you are ready to dive deeper into the pool of property management. The subsequent sections will focus on each of these principles in detail, explaining their intricacies, offering actionable steps, and providing practical examples from our experience in the rental real estate industry.

Chapter 4. Building a Fiscally Balanced Portfolio

Owning rental properties can be akin to sitting on a goldmine, if you know how to shrewdly build and manage your real estate portfolio. The real estate market, just like any other, is susceptible to fluctuations. Therefore, having a fiscally balanced portfolio helps to mitigate risks and capitalize on opportunities. In this chapter, we will delve into the various aspects of creating and managing a rewarding portfolio of rental properties.

4.1. How to Grow Your Portfolio

A common saying in real estate investing is "Your first deal is your most difficult." Once you have your first property under your belt, the confidence and experience you gain make the subsequent deals easier. Here are some ways to grow your portfolio:

1. Reinvest: The most effective way of growing your real estate portfolio is by reinvesting your profits. This might include using the rental income from your properties, or through flipping houses. The essence lies in making your earnings work for you.

2. Buy in Bulk: As you gain confidence as a landlord, consider buying multiple properties at once. Many real estate brokers offer discounts for bulk purchases. This requires substantial finance and property management skills, but equally provides a rapid expansion of your portfolio.

3. Partner up: If resources are limited, consider a partnership. Find a like-minded individual who aims to invest in real estate. This spreads the risk and financial requirements, making it more manageable to buy multiple properties.

However you choose to grow, ensure every addition aligns with your investment strategy and increases your portfolio's balance.

4.2. Building a Diverse Portfolio

A diverse portfolio is a healthy portfolio. As much as possible, avoid investing in the same property types located in the same geographic region. Any local economy's downturn could greatly affect your portfolio's performance.

1. Different Property Types: Invest in an assortment of properties, such as single-family homes, multi-family units, commercial properties, and mixed-use real estate. Each comes with its unique advantages and challenges, providing portfolio balance.

2. Different Locations: Geographic diversification helps cushion your portfolio against regional economic downturns. Spread your investments across different cities, states, or even countries.

3. Different Markets: Some landlords choose to spread the risk by investing in different types of markets, such as lower-income (but stable) neighborhoods, middle-class territories, or luxury markets.

The goal of diversification is to safeguard your portfolio against market chaos and give you multiple streams of income.

4.3. The Financial Side of Things

To thrive in any industry, a clear understanding of the financial side of things is crucial. Here's how to stay financially savvy:

1. Know Your Numbers: Knowledge of key financial indicators is vital in real estate. Metrics such as rental yield, cash flow, return on investment (ROI), and capitalization rate can help you make informed buying, selling, and renting decisions.

2. Financing: Many investors take advantage of financial leverage

while building their real estate portfolio. Loans can aid in buying properties without having to wait to accumulate the total purchase price, helping to accelerate growth.

3. Maintaining Cash Reserves: It's crucial to always have cash reserves to cater for unexpected expenses, like major repairs, vacancies, and market downturns. Being cash-rich helps you remain afloat.

4.4. Future-Proofing Your Portfolio

Another way to ensure a balanced portfolio is to future-proof it against potential market upheavals.

1. Flexibility: The real estate market is constantly evolving. Your portfolio should adapt to these changes timeously. Stay abreast of market trends, demographic shifts, and emerging property technologies.

2. Property Improvement: Regular upgrades and renovations keep your properties competitive, attract higher-paying tenants, and increase your property's value.

3. Sustainable properties: More and more renters are looking for eco-friendly living spaces. Finding innovative ways to 'green' your properties can future-proof them for a long-term return on your investments.

By following the principles outlined above, you can build a robust and balanced rental property portfolio. It positions you to weather financial storms while maintaining steady profit when the market is up. Remember, real estate investing is a marathon, not a sprint. Patience, sound decision-making, and consistent reinvestment are your keys to long-term success.

Chapter 5. The Art of Attracting and Retaining Tenants

Understanding your target market, their needs, and expectations is the first step in mastering the art of attracting and retaining tenants. This requires a multifaceted approach that goes beyond just advertising your property. It requires a deep understanding of the local market, ongoing maintenance and improvements, and earnest relationships with your tenants.

5.1. Knowing the Local Rental Market

The local rental market dictates the amount of rent you can reasonably ask for and the types of tenants you can attract. Thus, understanding the local market is crucial. Researching nearby rental prices will help you determine a competitive rent that will attract potential tenants. You can use online real estate platforms or ask a local realtor for a market assessment.

Moreover, discerning the demographic characteristics of renter-occupants within the area can provide useful insights into what potential tenants might be looking for. For example, an area dominated by university students will have different preferences from one that's home to many young families or retirees.

5.2. Marketing Your Property

Effectively marketing your property is a critical part of attracting tenants. This involves creating enticing adverts, which should be strategically featured on platforms that your target tenant demographic is most likely to utilize.

For your advertisements to stand out, invest in high-quality photos showcasing your property in the most appealing light. Highlight the key features that are attractive to your target demographic and specify any inclusive utilities, like water or gas.

5.3. Making Impressions Count

Your potential tenants' first impressions of your property could make or break their decision to rent. Therefore, strive to give them a positive first impression through well-managed property viewings, where you can highlight its compelling attributes.

Prioritize cleanliness and order for your property, and consider staging the house to help potential tenants visualize living there. This can go a long way in converting viewings into signed lease agreements.

5.4. Screening Your Tenants

Screening prospective tenants is an essential procedure that helps ensure you let your property to reliable individuals. Run background checks and credit reports to ascertain their reliability, and always ask for references — preferably from previous landlords. This prevents potential issues down the line, reducing the risk of property damage, late payments, or violation of lease agreements.

5.5. Cultivating Strong Landlord-Tenant Relationships

Maintaining a good relationship with your tenants is not just the ethical thing to do; it's good for business, too. Your communication with tenants should be respectful, responsive, and consistent. Quick action on repair requests, regular updates on any changes in property management, and clear communication on rent and utilities can foster a positive relationship between you and your tenants.

Remember to respect their privacy. Avoid unannounced visits and ensure you follow all applicable laws and regulations regarding entry into rented spaces.

5.6. Regular Maintenance and Improvements

Attending to regular maintenance is one of the surest ways of keeping your tenants satisfied. Regularly inspect the property for any issues that might need fixing — such as plumbing or electrical mishaps — and repair them promptly.

Also, consider periodic upgrades or improvements to the property. Features such as a fresh coat of paint, renewed appliances, or improved landscaping can boost the property's appeal and keep your tenants happy.

5.7. Renewing Lease Agreements

At the end of a lease term, consider whether you want to retain the current tenants or seek new ones. If you have reliable tenants, offering lease renewal can save you the effort and cost of finding new occupants. You might consider offering incentives, like a small discount on the first month's rent upon renewal, to encourage retention.

Rental property management is a delicate balance between maintaining your property, understanding your market, and fostering positive relationships with your tenants. Follow this guide to attract the right tenants for your property and retain them for as long as possible, building a profitable and enduring rental real estate venture.

Chapter 6. Demystifying Property Maintenance and Renovation

Understanding property maintenance and renovation is one of the first major steps an investor must take to ensure long-term success in the rental property business. While it may seem inconvenient at times, regular maintenance and strategic renovations can provide numerous benefits, including attracting more tenants, retaining tenants for longer periods, and even increasing the property's value.

6.1. The Basics of Property Maintenance

Property maintenance involves tasks designed to keep a property running smoothly. It ranges from routine inspections to repairs and updating outdated components. Ultimately, the goal is to maintain the property's longevity, safety, and usability.

Maintenance is typically categorized into two types: reactive maintenance, sometimes known as corrective or breakdown maintenance, and preventive maintenance.

Chapter 7. Reactive maintenance

Reactive maintenance entails responding to unforeseen breakdowns and making necessary repairs. This could range from repairing a broken pipe to a faulty furnace. It's vital to attend to these issues promptly, as letting them linger can cause more severe problems down the line.

Chapter 8. Preventive maintenance

Preventive maintenance involves regular check-ups and minor repairs aimed at preventing potential future problems. Regular tasks could involve checking the roof for leaks, inspecting HVAC systems, and optimizing the insulation.

While preventive maintenance can seem like an upfront cost, it often saves money in the long run by mitigating larger, costlier repairs.

8.1. Hiring Property Maintenance Services

While some landlords manage property maintenance themselves, many opt for hiring professional property maintenance services. Professionals bring expertise in various aspects of maintenance, which could save you time and avert potential oversights.

Hiring professionals also gives you more time to focus on growing your business, instead of being tied down by the day-to-day responsibilities of maintaining properties.

When considering property maintenance service providers, factors such as cost, scope of service, reliability, and expertise should be rigorously evaluated.

8.2. Tenant's Role in Property Maintenance

Tenants also play a substantial role in property maintenance. They are typically responsible for keeping the property clean, reporting any problems as soon as they arise, and taking necessary care not to cause unnecessary damage.

As a landlord, it's crucial to communicate these responsibilities to the tenant at the start of the lease, and regularly make sure your tenants are fulfilling their designated roles.

8.3. Leveraging Technology for Property Maintenance

In today's digital era, various tools and platforms can help optimize property maintenance. Property management software, for example, can remind you of scheduled maintenance tasks, allow tenants to report issues online, and even keep a log of past maintenance which can be helpful for future reference or in case of disputes.

8.4. When Renovations are Necessary

Occasionally, property maintenance alone is not enough. That's where renovations come in.

Property renovation aims to improve the property's value by replacing outdated features or reworking the property's layout to better meet modern demands.

However, whether to renovate is a decision that should be carefully thought out, considering factors like budget, return on investment, and the property's current condition. Renovations should ultimately increase the property's value or rental yield, whether immediately or in the long term.

8.5. The Renovation Process

Renovating a property is typically more involved than regular maintenance, so proper planning is key. It begins with an assessment of the current property's condition, identifying areas that could benefit most from renovation. This might involve hiring a professional property inspector, who can give a detailed rundown of what needs to be addressed.

Next, determine a budget for the renovation - it's essential to keep spending under control to ensure the renovation still yields profit.

Once the groundwork is laid, the work begins. This could mean anything from updating a kitchen, adding energy-efficient windows, to overhauling the entire floor plan.

Remember, the best renovations are those that add real value to the property, not just aesthetic enhancements.

8.6. Renovation Payoffs

Intelligent renovations can transform a rental property and significantly increase its rental yield or resale value. Some renovations, like adding extra rooms or modernizing kitchens and bathrooms, can attract a higher caliber of tenant willing to pay more for these improvements.

Remember, it is crucial to balance the cost of a renovation against the expected return. You don't want to overspend on a fancy overhaul that won't drastically increase the rental yield.

Understanding property maintenance and renovation is a process, and it's okay not to know everything at the outset. The goal is to build a solid foundation and then add pieces as you learn and grow.

In the end, a well-maintained and prudently renovated property can boost your real estate rental business by attracting and retaining higher-quality tenants, thus securing higher yields and, consequently, escalating your wealth in rental real estate.

Chapter 9. Effective Legal Practices and Rental Laws

Understanding and abiding by the rental laws and legal practices can daunting, but it's a cornerstone to any successful real estate rental business. Property owners need to navigate a tangle of local, state and federal laws that impact everything from tenant screening to property maintenance to eviction procedures.

9.1. Landlord-Tenant Laws

The crux to any successful rental property business centers on the landlord-tenant relationship, bound by various tenant-right laws along with responsibilities and duties of both parties.

Laws vary considerably across regions; therefore, educating oneself about local, state, and federal laws is cardinal for avoiding legal entanglements. American landlords, for instance, need to be acquainted with laws such as the Fair Housing Act (FHA), which prohibits discriminatory practices based on sex, race, color, religion, disability, familial status or national origin.

It's also worth noting that some states implement rent control or stabilization laws to protect tenants from exorbitant rental hikes. Moreover, most landlord-tenant laws cover the following areas:

- Rent: The terms of rent amount, frequency, due date, and penalties for late payments and non-payments overall.

- Security Deposits: The deposit alterations, return, deductions, and relevant timelines are essential.

- Repairs: The duty of the landlord to provide a habitable dwelling and facilitate necessary repairs.

- Rental Agreements: The terms outlined in a lease or rental agreement, which define the rights and responsibilities of both parties are of prime importance.

9.2. Eviction Laws

Evictions can be a challenging inevitability within the property rental business. Handling evictions meticulously following all the legal regulations is essential to avoid further penalties. Each state has specific laws regarding the process, often inclusive of:

- Initial Notice: Landlords must serve an eviction notice to the tenant, giving them a chance to rectify the issue or vacate the premises.

- Legal Grounds: There should be a legal violation of the rental or lease agreement by the tenant, warranting eviction.

- Court Proceedings: Failure of the tenant to comply may lead to a lawsuit.

Forethought, appropriate documentation, and humane treatment during the eviction process can prevent miring in legal challenges and foster goodwill with the broader community.

9.3. Fair Housing Act

Implemented in 1968, the U.S. Fair Housing Act (FHA) is a federal law that proscribes discrimination in housing based on color, race, religion, national origin, sex, disability, and familial status. The FHA covers most housing types, although there are some exclusions.

Breaching the FHA can result in serious penalties. Therefore, property managers need to ensure their policies, practices, advertising, and interactions with tenants and potential tenants do not discriminate based on the protected categories mentioned above.

9.4. Americans with Disabilities Act

Another cogent law rental property owners must understand is the Americans with Disabilities Act of 1990. This legislation prohibits discrimination against individuals with disabilities in all areas of public life, including jobs, schools, transportation, and all public and private places.

According to the Act, landlords cannot refuse to rent to a person solely because of their disability. They are also legally obligated to make reasonable accommodations for such tenants. For example, a landlord might need to modify policies or services to provide equal opportunity for a tenant with a disability. There might also be responsibilities for physical modifications to the property to ensure accessibility.

9.5. Property Maintenance Laws

Property owners are legally obligated to provide safe, clean, and habitable living conditions for their tenants. Property laws mandate that landlords promptly address necessary repairs and maintain livable conditions. Failure to do so could render the landlord legally and financially responsible for any damages or injuries incurred due to negligence.

9.6. The Importance of Legal Assistance

Even with a firm understanding of laws and regulations, the complexity of real estate law warrants professional advice. Retaining a real estate attorney can save property managers time, money, and protect their business from potential legal debacles.

Your attorney will advise on intricacies of different laws, lease agreements, property maintenance, tenant screening, evictions, and more. They can also review, update, or draft any necessary documentation to meet legal requirements, protect your rights as a landlord, and mitigate potential liabilities.

In conclusion, operating a rental property business necessitates compliance with a variety of complex laws and legal practices and non-adherence can result in severe repercussions. Therefore, a combination of understanding the crucial elements of these laws, regular compliance checks and updates, and obtaining professional legal advice provides the best methodology to navigate this challenging yet crucial aspect of property management. With sound legal practices, you can have a thriving, profitable, and legally safeguarded rental property business.

Chapter 10. The Role of Technology in Property Management

Undeniably, the evolution of technology over the years has impacted various domains, including the property management sector. Modern technology is paving the way for property managers to increase operational efficiency drastically, provide seamless tenant services, and improve the profitability of rental real estate properties.

10.1. Digital Marketing and Property Advertising

In the technologically advanced era, digital marketing and online advertisements have become the go-to strategy for property managers seeking potential tenants. Modern property management software provides options to create customizable ads, making it easier to attract the right renters. These platforms facilitate the use of professional and eye-catching templates, allowing property managers to give their properties a noteworthy online presence.

Moreover, these platforms also offer the utility to automatically publish the ad across multiple listing sites, boosting visibility and attracting more prospects. Prospective tenants have entirely moved online for their housing search, thus making digital marketing a fundamental tool in property management.

10.2. Online Tenant Applications and Screening

With advanced property management technologies, gone are the days of manual, paper-based tenant application and screening processes. Online applications allow prospective tenants to apply at their convenience, increasing the pool of applicants. In addition, many platforms integrate background and credit checks, facilitating quicker and more detailed tenant screening and reducing the probability of bad rentals.

Moreover, these technologies can store and organize tenant applications, making it easier to retrieve when needed. This digitalized approach prevents the loss of crucial information and keeps the process transparent and manageable.

10.3. Property Management Software

Property management software is revolutionizing the rental real estate sector by offering an array of features ranging from accounting solutions to maintenance management. This technology gives property managers the ability to automate repetitive tasks, therefore freeing up time to focus on strategic activities that grow their portfolios.

This software facilitates efficient bookkeeping by automating rent collection, expense tracking, and providing custom reports. Consequently, property managers can make sound financial decisions based on real-time data. Furthermore, the software offers adequate solutions for better maintenance management. They provide features such as automated notifications to inform property managers about upcoming repairs and allow tracking of ongoing maintenance tasks.

10.4. Use of AI and Chatbots

Artificial Intelligence (AI) and chatbots are taking customer service to a whole new level in property management. These technologies can handle routine queries, schedule appointments, and keep track of maintenance requests round the clock. This ensures residents receive immediate responses, improving tenant satisfaction and reducing the likelihood of vacancies.

AI and chatbots also help in predictive maintenance. They use predictive analytics to determine when assets may need maintenance or replacement. This approach reduces unexpected expenses, prolonging the useful life of these assets and improving the property's overall profitability.

10.5. IoT and Smart Home Technology

Internet of Things (IoT) and smart home technology have altered how property managers and landlords manage their properties. With smart devices such as security cameras, leak detectors, and energy-saving appliances, property management has become more convenient and cost-effective.

By using these devices, property managers can monitor their properties in real-time, preventing mishaps and malfunctions. Additionally, these technologies reduce utility costs and environmental impact through optimized energy usage, contributing to sustainable property management.

Overall, technology plays an indispensable role in property management. With the advancement in technology, we can foresee a bright future with many more opportunities for both property managers and property investors to maximize wealth through real estate rentals. It makes the once daunting task of managing rentals a breeze while simultaneously providing a seamless experience for tenants and ensuring that the property remains in its best condition.

Chapter 11. Risk Management and Insurance Essentials

In the dynamic universe of real estate rentals, risk is a constant player. Hence, managing it becomes crucial to safe guard the precious investments and to ensure a steady flow of profits. This chapter focuses on the essentials of risk management and its insurance dimension in the rental real estate context.

11.1. Risk Management Essentials

Every potential investment comes with its own set of risks. Rental properties are no exception. Having a reliable risk management strategy in place can help keep your investments safe and successful. One primary aspect of risk management is to identify potential threats and prepare a contingency plan.

1. **Damage to Property**: Possible damage to the rental property, whether from natural disasters, tenant behaviour, or other external influences, is a significant risk landlords face. It could disrupt the rental income flow and require unplanned spending for repairs.

2. **Loss of Income**: This could occur due to extended vacancies, tenant default, disputes, or eviction processes, leading to a significant impact on the regular cash flow.

3. **Liability Issues**: Accidents can happen on the rented premise, and as a landlord, you might be held liable, leading to legal disputes or compensation claims.

4. **Market Fluctuations**: Changes in market dynamics like property prices, tenant demand, or rental rates can affect the profitability of the rental income.

Each identified risk calls for specific preventive measures and controls, be it regular property maintenance, robust tenant screening processes, premium legal and insurance coverage, or vigilant market tracking.

11.2. Insurance Essentials

Insurance plays a key role as a financial buffer against the major risks in the rental property business. Knowing the types of insurance available and what they cover is the cornerstone of a robust risk management strategy.

1. **Landlord Insurance**: This insurance covers property damage caused by natural calamities like fires or storms and tenant-related damages. It also provides coverage for loss of rent due to landlord-tenant disputes or property damage.

2. **Liability Insurance**: This is designed to protect landlords from the financial fallout of legal claims arising from injuries or accidents that occur on the rental property.

3. **Income Protection Insurance**: This type of policy guards landlords against the loss of rental income, possibly due to tenant default, vacancy periods or disputes.

Navigating the complexities of insurance can be challenging. Here are a few key things to keep in mind:

- Understand What's Covered: Not all policies protect against every risk. Ensure to read the policy terms thoroughly, and understand what's covered and what's not.

- Consider the Property Location: The location of your rental property may impact the cost and type of coverage needed. Natural disaster-prone areas might need more comprehensive coverage, while properties in safe, urban areas could cost less to insure.

- Ensure Adequate Coverage: It's important to ensure that your policy coverage limits are high enough to cover the potential costs you might face. Factor in the replacement cost of the property, potential liability expenses, and loss of rental income.

- Review and Update Regularly: Changes in the property, tenants, or market conditions might warrant a change in policy. Regularly review and update your insurance policies to ensure they remain relevant and effective.

Insurance is an investment, not an expense. Through effective risk management and relevant insurance, landlords can protect their investment and guarantee a steady rental income, turning their property into a profitable enterprise in the long run. The security it offers against possible adversities makes it an indispensable part of the wealth creation journey in real estate rentals. As the adage goes, "Hope for the best, prepare for the worst." These essentials will help you do just that. Happy investing!

Don't forget, there's no universal blueprint for risk management and insurance. What works for others might not work for you. Regular evaluation and fine-tuning of the strategy and policies can lead towards a safe, rewarding, and prosperous journey in the rental property industry.

Chapter 12. Exploring the Power of Real Estate Tax Benefits

Nestled within the realm of real estate investments are a multitude of tax benefits that can provide a significant boost to your financial wealth, if harnessed correctly. These benefits, often overlooked by novice investors, can render real estate investment one of the most lucrative sectors for savvy business minds.

12.1. Understanding the Basics

The United States tax code dramatically favours real estate investors by offering a host of tax deductions, credits, and loopholes that could potentially save thousands of dollars yearly. Understanding these tax advantages is an essential first step to exploring the power of real estate tax benefits fully.

Before jumping into the myriad advantages, it's important to understand how real estate tax is pinned against your income. The U.S. Internal Revenue Service (IRS) considers rental income as part of your overall annual earnings, meaning you need to report it on your tax return. However, the real estate taxes you pay on your property annually can be deducted from your income taxes - a factor that greatly aids in offsetting potential losses.

12.2. Navigating Capital Gains Tax

Capital gains tax is levied on the profit you make from selling your investment property. Yet, the tax code holds provisions that may allow you to control, reduce, or even fully eliminate this tax:

- The 1031 Exchange: This rule allows investors to defer paying capital gains tax if the profits from the property sale are reinvested into a like-kind property. The reinvestment should occur within 180 days of the sale to qualify. To navigate this process seamlessly, it's recommended to engage a Qualified Intermediary.

- Primary Residence Exclusion: If you lived in your rental property for at least 2 out of the last 5 years before selling it, you may qualify for the Primary Residence Exclusion rule. This allows for an individual to exclude up to $250,000 ($500,000 for married couples filing jointly) in capital gains from tax.

12.3. Unpacking Depreciation

Depreciation is the method by which the IRS allows you to deduct the cost of buying or improving a rental property, spread across the asset's useful life, typically 27.5 years for residential property. You'll be able to write off a portion of your investment each year, reducing your taxable rental income.

However, when you sell the property, you may have to pay a recapture tax on the depreciation claimed. This is where strategies such as the 1031 Exchange can be valuable in deferring this potential tax.

12.4. Mortgage Interest and Other Expense Deductions

Interest that accrues on a mortgage tied to a rental property is 100% tax-deductible. This includes any interest paid on a loan used to buy, build, or improve the property. In addition to mortgage interest, other operating expenses applicable to the rental property are also deductible. These can include property management fees, repairs, maintenance, property taxes, insurance, and even travel costs related to property management.

12.5. Real Estate Professional Status (REPS)

If you can qualify as a Real Estate Professional, you may be able to deduct your real estate losses against other types of income, which is otherwise restricted. REPS is an IRS defined status that requires you to meet certain specific qualifications, such as spending more than half of your working hours and at least 750 hours per year materially participating in real estate as a developer, broker, landlord or the like.

12.6. Utilizing the Passive Activity Loss Rule

The Passive Activity Loss rule allows investors to deduct up to $25,000 in losses on rental real estate against other income sources. However, it's subject to restrictions, including a phase-out that reduces the deduction if your modified adjusted gross income is between $100,000 and $150,000.

12.7. Utilizing a Self-Directed IRA

A Self-Directed Individual Retirement Account (SDIRA) allows you to invest in a broader set of assets, including real estate. The income generated in an SDIRA is tax-sheltered until withdrawal after the age of 59.5, allowing your real estate profits to grow tax-deferred.

12.8. Opportunity Zones

Investing in designated Opportunity Zones can offer significant tax advantages. Investors can defer capital gains tax when they invest those gains into Qualified Opportunity Funds. Further, if these opportunity funds are held for a long enough period, potential profits from them can be tax-free.

What we've outlined here only scratches the surface of tax benefits offered by real estate investments. Each investor's circumstances are different, and so will be their approach to mitigate taxes. It's highly recommended to involve a competent tax advisor or accountant who understands real estate taxation in your long-term investment strategy. They can help identify all the tax-saving opportunities available to you, ensuring you squeeze the most profit out of your real estate investments. Above all, understanding and properly leveraging these tax benefits can open a gateway to maximizing wealth in real estate rentals like never before.

Chapter 13. Strategies for Portfolio Expansion and Profit Maximization

Expanding your real estate portfolio and maximizing your profits involves diverse strategies that go beyond simply buying more properties. Success in this area requires understanding market trends, considering various types of real estate, managing your finances wisely, and considering your long-term goals.

13.1. Market Research

Start by researching the local rental real estate market and understanding the trends. This research should include analyzing housing prices, the rental demand, expected changes in the population, and local economic conditions.

You can study the local market conditions through online research, attending industry events, networking with other landlords, or having a chat with local real estate agents. By being in sync with the economic situation and your local market, you can make informed decisions about where and when to invest.

13.2. Property-Type Consideration

Different property types serve different kinds of tenants and generate diverse streams of income. The common property types include single-family homes, multi-family homes, condos, and commercial properties.

Remember that each category has its unique benefits, challenges, and market dynamics which affects its respective profitability. For example, while single-family homes often have stable tenants, condos might offer better cash flow due to their locations.

To decide on the property type to invest in, define your goals and the kind of landlord you want to be. Align these objectives with your risk tolerance, your aptitude for property management, availability of the properties, and the kind of tenants you're ready to deal with.

13.3. Financial Management

Your financial strategy directly affects your ability to expand your portfolio and the success of your rental property business. Wise financial management often starts with a thorough understanding of all your costs. Mortgage, insurance, taxes, utilities, property management, maintenance and repairs – all these expenses should be factored into your rental rates and your long-term financial plan.

Also, ensure you set up an emergency fund dedicated to your rental properties to cover unexpected costs. This fund safeguards your portfolio in cases of significant repairs or periods of vacancies.

Equally important is the step to diversify your real estate investments. Diversification helps protect your investments from localized market downturns. It might mean investing in different types of properties, different regions, or even thinking beyond real estate, such as equities or bonds.

13.4. Long-Term Planning

Real estate is a long-term game. You have to think points ahead and consider aspects like depreciation, tax advantages, rent increases, and capital growth. Regularly reassess your real estate strategy and investment portfolio to keep them in line with the changing market conditions and your evolving personal and financial situations.

Consider future-proofing your investments as part of your long-term plan. Ensuring the properties are environmentally sustainable and equipped with the technology required by modern tenants can significantly increase the rental appeal and future-proof the property's revenue.

13.5. Profit Maximization Strategies

Profit maximization in rental real estate may require implementing creative strategies. For instance, consider adding services like cleaning or landscaping for an additional charge. The increase in revenue from these services can significantly boost your profits.

Regularly review your rents with the prevailing market rates and adjust them appropriately. In the right circumstances, rent increases can provide a significant boost to your profits without driving away good tenants.

Lastly, consider reinvesting the income generated from your investments back into your portfolio through regular property upgrades or purchasing additional properties. This strategy continues the virtuous cycle of portfolio expansion and profit maximization.

13.6. Conclusion

Curating a portfolio in real estate is an art cultivated through abundant caution, calculated risks, and a touch of creativity. It's crucial to maintain a long-term perspective and adapt to evolving scenarios. Conversely, wise financial management, regular market research, right property selection, and innovative profit maximization strategies can prove pivotal in your ambition to expand the real estate portfolio and amplify profits.

This industry, deluged with wealth-building opportunities, is all about seizing the right ones. Sow the seeds of strategic decisions, and in due course, you'll reap the benefits of blooming profits. Embark this compelling journey of property rental, sustaining through the tempests, navigating towards the rainbows, and accumulating a pot of gold in the process. Over time, the bricks you bought will churn out golden returns, making your wealth graph an envy to many. It's time to make that lucrative leap – the realm of riches awaits!

Stay open to newer knowledge, burgeoning trends, unstoppable growth, and strike when opportunities knock. Strategize, diversify, and monetize in real estate rentals – after all, it's the sunrise industry that never truly sets.